# Wherever He Leads

**LOIS PATRICK**

Wherever He Leads
Published by Lois Patrick
with Castle Publishing Ltd
New Zealand

© 2021 Lois Patrick
loispatrick9@gmail.com

ISBN 978-0-473-58673-7 (Softcover)
ISBN 978-0-473-58674-4 (ePUB)
ISBN 978-0-473-58675-1 (Kindle)

Production & Typesetting:
Andrew Killick
Castle Publishing Services
www.castlepublishing.co.nz

Photographs:
Lois Patrick

Cover Design:
Paul Smith

Thanks to Glenys Knopp for
her careful editing of the manuscript.

Unless otherwise stated, all scriptures taken from
the Holy Bible, New International Version®, NIV®.
Copyright © 1973, 1978, 1984, 2011 by Biblica, Inc.™
Used by permission of Zondervan.
All rights reserved worldwide.

ALL RIGHTS RESERVED

No part of this publication may be reproduced,
stored in a retrieval system, or transmitted
in any form or by any means, electronic, mechanical,
photocopying, recording or otherwise,
without prior written permission from the author.

*These reflections model a frank interaction of faith, life and scripture. Lois Patrick has done us all a service in her honest exploration of life's ups and downs – its challenges to faith, its moments of insight, and the opportunities to experience grace. Each short chapter brings life and scripture together in ways from which all Christians can learn. Here is the word of God made living and real in the midst of sorrow, excitement and challenge. For New Zealanders, there is the added bonus that these are our places – names we recognise, situations we understand. At times we are presented with searching questions which remind us that scripture itself does not let us settle for easy answers but calls us to new steps of faith as we seek to follow and 'to see the God who sees us'. Highly recommended.*

– Martin Sutherland, Senior Research Fellow, Laidlaw College

*As a counsellor, I have spent many years with people of faith struggling to know where God is for them in their current situations. Lois has used her own experiences, many that my clients could easily identify with. Into those experiences she brings to life scripture that is relevant and gives hope and comfort. It's a wonderful read. It's encouraging and real; a must-have book.*

– Chris Hight, Counsellor

*Life is not a journey to eternity
with the intention of arriving safely
in a pretty, well-preserved body,
but instead to skid in broadside,
thoroughly used up,
totally worn out,
and loudly proclaiming 'Wow, what a ride!'*

*– Author unknown*

# Contents

| | |
|---|---|
| Introduction | 9 |
| Coming Home | 11 |
| Changing Seasons | 15 |
| Do You Love Me? | 18 |
| How Long, Lord? | 21 |
| Have Your Ears Been Pierced? | 25 |
| Building Altars | 28 |
| Quit Quarrelling | 33 |
| Waiting for Eagles Wings | 36 |
| Tangiwai and Tears | 40 |
| Get Out of Your Boat! | 43 |
| Leaving a Legacy | 47 |
| A Voice in the Night | 50 |
| Adopted Into the Family | 55 |
| Relinquishing a Dream | 58 |
| Are You Tired and Worn Out? | 62 |
| Tested by Fire | 66 |
| Wearing a Mask | 70 |
| A Day to Remember | 73 |
| Earthquakes and Aftershocks | 77 |
| Doing or Being? | 80 |
| Hang in There | 84 |
| How Will this Journey End? | 87 |

# Introduction

We have spent many hours exploring the high-country roads in the South Island of New Zealand. The road conditions vary from well-graded gravel roads to rock-strewn narrow tracks. Some lead us through lush valleys, others take us high into the mountains.

Regardless of the state of the roads, the scenery is breathtaking. The challenge of the difficult terrain only makes the trip more exhilarating. Being a passenger, I am committed to going wherever the driver takes me! By nightfall we are tired, but energised by the fact we made it safely home.

Life is a journey. God is in the driver's seat; we are the passengers – committed to going wherever He leads us.

May the following pages be an encouragement as you face the challenges of living in today's world.

With God's 'ever-present help', may you be able to say of your journey: *'Wow, what a ride!'*

# Coming Home
*There is no place quite like home*

2020 was the year everyone wanted to come home!

As the global pandemic spread around the world, affecting millions of people, there was a rush to go back to the safety of home.

New Zealand was regarded as a safe country and we saw thousands of ex-pat kiwis returning to our shores.

But many were unable to return. As our borders closed, we heard of those stranded in foreign countries, unable to get flights home. Have you been in that position when all you wanted was to go home, but were denied the opportunity?

In Genesis 16:1-16, we read about a woman who had reached breaking point and just wanted to return to her home. An Egyptian slave girl named Hagar belonged to Sarai, wife of Abram. She had no choice but to become a surrogate mother to provide a child for the couple.

But once Hagar had conceived, things turned unpleasant between her and Sarai. With Abram's blessing, Sarai became cruel and abusive, mistreating Hagar until the slave girl, in desperation, ran away and headed for home.

Alone and confused, she finally stopped to rest beside a spring in the desert. It was here that an angel of God found her and asked: 'Hagar, what are you doing here?'

She replied honestly, 'I'm running away from Sarai, my mistress.'

How often have you and I been in that same place – running

away? Maybe not in a physical sense, but in our hearts, we want to turn our backs on the situation in which we find ourselves. The easiest way out is to give up and 'run away'.

Unfortunately, our problems seem to accompany us wherever we go and we only have ourselves for company! That may seem like a good solution, but it's facing our problems and working through them that makes us strong.

The Angel of God knew Hagar's situation. Did you notice he called her by name? Hagar. That's something neither Sarai nor Abram did. They referred to her as 'the maid'.

What was God's word to Hagar? First, a question: 'Where have you come from and where are you going?'

Notice Hagar answered the first part of the question but not the last. 'I'm running away' – but no comment as to where she was going. So often we focus on the past and have no plan for the future. All we want to do is escape the situation we are in.

What was God's instruction to Hagar? 'Go back to your mistress!'

Along with the command to return came His promise for the future. From being lonely, scared, rejected and abused, Hagar became a different woman. Her response was: 'You are the God who sees me,' for she said, 'I have now seen the One who sees me.'

There lies the answer.

*God sees us, but we also need to see Him.*

Our God is the same God who saw Hagar in her distress. Our God is a God who sees. He sees us, whatever our situation. He sees and He cares. He knows what is best for us.

In your present situation, have you 'seen the God who sees you'? Instead of running, take time to pause and listen for His 'still, small voice' during the storm.

*Coming Home*

How did Hagar feel as she turned and made her way back to Sarai? She returned with a different understanding of her circumstances. She now had God's promise that He was with her and had her future in His hands.

Have you seen the God who sees you?

He saw Hagar in her distress. He also sees you.

Stop running, pause, listen. Hear what God is saying to you regarding your present situation.

*Read Genesis 16 and 21:1-19*

# Changing Seasons

I love the changes that come with each season. The heat of summer giving way to the dramatic colours of autumn. The snow disappearing from the mountains (or the backyard!) and the spring bulbs bravely sending up tiny shoots to become a splash of colour in a grey world.

*He has made everything beautiful in its time. (Ecclesiastes 3:11)*

Imagine what life would be like without the different seasons. An endless spring when the new buds never bloomed, or a never-ending summer with no refreshing autumn rain. Autumn is a beautiful harvest time, but then the ground needs to lie fallow ready for replanting. Winter has a beauty all its own, but could we live with the continuous cold, maybe even snow and ice?

While we can enjoy the changing seasons of nature, we are not always so thrilled as the seasons of our life change. Life does not always follow the same order as nature's seasons. We may be enjoying the warm summer, or the newness of spring, when suddenly our whole world can be turned upside down, and we find ourselves in a winter season.

How do you cope with the changing seasons? A friend experienced the sudden loss of her husband through a tragic car accident. The attending police officer said, 'He was in the wrong place at the wrong time.' As the reality set in, my friend replied, 'No, he was in the right place in God's time.' A fantastic response, which could only come from a deep faith in God's care and timing.

I am fascinated by the life of the majestic eagle. There is a season in its life when it must face change. At around forty years of age, an eagle will fly to a nest high in the mountains, where it will begin to knock its beak against a rock until it is worn away, allowing a new beak to grow. Then it plucks away at its talons, so they too can regrow and finally, it will pluck out and regrow all its feathers. This whole process can take nearly six months. What an arduous change, but it enables the eagle to live for another thirty to forty years.

How hard is it to accept change? We all like to see progress, but do we want to change our ways to ensure it happens?

There are times when change is worth fighting for. In Genesis 32:24-32, we find God dealing with Jacob, putting him through a traumatic experience. Jacob was alone in the dark, wondering if his brother would accept his gifts or would he kill him? Suddenly a man appeared and wrestled him to the ground. It didn't take Jacob long to realise this was a man from God. It was a long, hard struggle before the man changed Jacob's name to Israel. His encounter with God resulted in Jacob limping away but knowing God's blessing.

There will be times when we wrestle with God. He wants us to grow strong and face life victoriously. Don't give up until you know God's blessing. Are you facing a new season in your life? Are you brave enough to let go of the old and embrace something new?

> *Remember not the former things, nor consider the things of old. Behold, I am doing a new thing; now it springs forth, do you not perceive it? I will make a way in the wilderness and rivers in the desert. (Isaiah 43:18-19 ESV)*

*The Lord himself goes before you and will be with you; He will never leave you nor forsake you. (Deuteronomy 31:8)*

**Changing Seasons**
*I find my life too, follows the seasons*
*Summer to autumn, winter to spring...*
*Why do I suddenly, and without reason*
*Find summer becomes winter*
*With nothing between*
*Or spring turns to autumn*
*And I lose summer's dream?*
*I only know God has a reason*
*And He walks with me through every season.*

*Why must my heart be frozen in winter*
*Weighed down by cares too heavy to bear*
*Facing life with no hope for tomorrow*
*Feeling only dread, pain and sorrow?*
*What comfort to know God has a reason*
*And holds my hand through every season.*

*Summer with all its laughter and freedom*
*Autumn with changes and future uncertain.*
*Soft spring showers after winter's slow thaw*
*Each with a purpose, neither hurried nor slow,*
*I'm content in the knowledge that God has a reason*
*As He walks me through each changing season.*

# Do You Love Me?

Jesus asked that question of Peter – three times!

I wonder what went through Peter's mind as he contemplated an answer. He had a very impulsive nature. Maybe he didn't stop to think and just blurted out, 'You know I love you, Lord.'

By the time the Lord asked him a third time, Peter was getting the point. Three times he had denied knowing Jesus. Three times he was asked, 'Do you love Me?'

How can we measure our love for the Lord? Put yourself in Peter's place.

How would you have answered those questions? Is yours an all-consuming love that will go to any lengths, make any sacrifice, even lay your life on the line?

Some years ago, we had the opportunity to go into China. Before boarding the train to Guangzhou, we were given the address of Pastor Samuel Lamb of the Underground Church, with strict instructions not to ask directions from the hotel staff, in case we were followed. Our rickshaw driver would not take us to the actual street but dropped us off and pointed across the Square.

The street we found was crowded, dirty and only big enough for bikes or a rickshaw. As we made our way up a narrow stone stairway, we were aware that everyone going in or out was being watched by the authorities.

It was there in a small third-floor room that we met Samuel Lamb and listened for an hour or two, as he told us about his church and his personal story.

His church building and the members were constantly under surveillance. The police regularly searched their houses. Each time the police visited the church, all their Bibles, hymn books, sound system etc., were confiscated. With great joy, Samuel told us, 'Before confiscation 900 people at church, after confiscation 1200!'

In that tiny cramped upstairs room, the house church held four services each week, always under the watchful eye of the authorities, always in danger of persecution.

Samuel told us of his studies through the Moody Bible Institute in Chicago, which he had not completed due to imprisonment. We had a simple ballpoint pen with us, which we had acquired while at Moody Bible Institute, some weeks earlier. He was so thrilled to be given it. It was like giving him his graduation gift!

What a humbling experience to hear his story. The Chinese government wanted him to register his church with them, but he refused. For this, he was sent to prison for more than twenty years. Fifteen years were spent in hard physical labour in the coal mines after he was found making a copy of the New Testament.

His father died seven years before his release, his wife two years before and his mother eleven months after.

When released from prison, he started preaching again, and the church grew. The authorities came back, confiscated all the Bibles, and arrested Pastor Lamb. He was interrogated and tortured for three days and told to close down the church.

What happened? He told his congregation that the police had said not to come back. The following Sunday, the attendance had doubled! The house church continued to hold four services each week, with between four to five thousand attending. How they managed to fit so many into that cramped apartment, I will never understand.

Pastor Samuel Lamb was threatened, beaten, and tortured for sharing the gospel, but at 66 years of age, he looked at us with a huge smile and said:

> 'I've been in prison twice; I'm ready for the third. I am so in love with my Saviour.'

In 2013, Pastor Samuel Lamb died. The press reported that the streets were crammed with over 30,000 people as they headed to the cemetery to mourn the life of a man whose love for his Saviour was the determining factor in all he did and said.

What a privilege to spend time with such a man of God.

I was left with a burning question: 'How much do I love my Saviour?'

# How Long, Lord?

I love Habakkuk. He is honest and comes straight to the point: 'God, I've got a complaint.'

The first chapter is full of questions and anger. He was frustrated with God, wanting to know how long the current situation was going to last.

Are you asking the same questions that Habakkuk was asking? 'Why are you allowing this?' 'How long will this go on for?'

The name Habakkuk means 'to embrace'. God wanted him to embrace his situation.

God's answer (Habakkuk 1:5-11) was not what Habakkuk wanted to hear.

*'I have an answer, but you won't believe it! It's going to get worse before it gets better.'*

Habakkuk was confused. The Babylonians were a godless nation, wicked and cruel, bringing violence and destruction wherever they invaded. How could God allow that to happen? How could He stand back and let such wickedness and suffering continue?

While God may seem silent and uninvolved in our world, He always has a plan to deal with evil and always works out justice eventually.

God is asking Habakkuk, 'What if things get worse before they get better? How will you cope?'

We have no idea what is ahead of us. What if our present situation does get worse before it gets better? Can we embrace our present situation in the same way?

Habakkuk doesn't know what to say to the people, so he says nothing. He went to his watchtower and waited. He knew he needed to be quiet and listen to what God had to say.

We need to learn what it means to 'be still and know that I am God' (Isaiah 46:10).

> *The one thing I ask of the Lord – the thing I seek most, is to live in the house of the Lord all the days of my life, delighting in the Lord's perfections and meditating in his Temple. For he will* **conceal me there when troubles come**; *he will hide me in his sanctuary. He will place me out of reach on a high rock.*
> *(Psalm 27:4-5 NLT)*

When Habakkuk was quiet and waiting, God answered, telling him to stop talking and start writing. God was saying, 'I know what I'm doing' (Habakkuk 2:2).

The righteous live by faith, not by feelings (Habakkuk 3:5). Is your life controlled by fear or faith? When faced with a situation we can't control, God asks us to embrace it, not to fight it.

Habakkuk chapter 2 can be depressing reading, but verse 20 is reassuring. God is in the heavens maintaining His absolute control!

As a result, we find Habakkuk is on his knees. 'I tremble but I will wait' (Habakkuk 3:16).

He's resigned to God's will and can finally say, 'Even though the fig tree does not blossom, there are no grapes on the vine, the olive crops fail. The fields lie empty and barren; the flocks die in the fields, the cattle barns are empty – Yet I will rejoice in the Lord. I will take joy in the God of my salvation' (Habakkuk 3:17,18).

*How Long, Lord?*

When there was nothing left, he would still rejoice. Can you say that even if your situation gets worse before it improves, you will put your trust in God and rejoice in whatever happens?

Habakkuk uses the word for a female deer. The hind's rear feet land in the same spot as the front feet have been. They are the most sure-footed of all mountain animals. They can reach the mountain tops with ease.

*The Sovereign LORD is my strength; he makes my feet like the feet of a deer. He enables me to tread on the heights. (Habakkuk 3:19)*

*He makes my feet like hinds' feet, and sets me upon high places. (Psalm 18:33 NASB)*

Are you like Habakkuk – embracing your situation with rejoicing? Are you 'as sure-footed as the deer with your feet on the mountain top'?

# Have Your Ears Been Pierced?

Have you had your ears pierced? It's a straightforward procedure, but it can be painful for some people. I wonder how you found the experience?

Did you know it was carried out a long time before it became fashionable for our generation?

Have you considered having a 'spiritual ear piercing'?

*Sacrifice and offering you did not desire, but my ears you have pierced; burnt offerings and sin offerings you did not require... I desire to do your will, O my God. (Psalm 40:6-8)*

Why does the psalmist say God did not require offerings and sacrifices? It was because David desired to do God's will, and 'his ears had been pierced.'

To understand this passage, we need to read Exodus 21:1-6,

*When you buy a Hebrew slave, he shall serve six years, and in the seventh, he shall go out free, for nothing... But if the slave plainly says, 'I love my master, my wife, and my children; I will not go out free,' then his master must take him before the judges, and he shall bring him to the door or the doorpost. And his master shall bore his ear through with an awl, and he shall be his slave forever. (ESV)*

These instructions also appear in Deuteronomy 15: 16-18.

The law stipulated that in the Sabbath year, a servant was to be set free. Having served for six years, they were able to leave and become a free man or woman. If they had been well treated and loved their master, the slaves may decide to stay. If this was their choice, they would stand by the doorpost and have an ear pierced with an awl, as a sign that they belonged to their master forever.

This early ear piercing came from a servant's love for his master. There was no pressure to do this, it was a voluntary decision, and it was a life-long commitment. There would be no questions about his future. The servant agreed to do all that his master asked of him.

We are also free to choose. Is our love for the Master deep enough to decide to be a lifetime servant? Have you had your ear pierced? Not physically, but figuratively: by committing your life to serve God whatever He asks you to do. You will be willing to obey, knowing the Master has the best plan for your life.

We cannot serve God if we just think it's the right thing to do, or we are afraid of consequences if we don't. Our service must arise out of love. Has the thought of having your 'ears pierced' caused you to turn away from serving God? Is the sacrifice too difficult to make?

We find a similar word in 1 Samuel 15:22,

> Samuel replied, 'Has the Lord as much pleasure in your burnt offerings and sacrifices as in your obedience? Obedience is far better than sacrifice. He is much more interested in your listening to him than in your offering the fat of rams to him.' (TLB)

Samuel was comparing sacrifices and obedience. He was not saying sacrifices were wrong, but in comparison, obedience was far better.

*Have Your Ears Been Pierced?*

Sacrificing an animal on the altar could become a ritual with little meaning, whereas obeying God would be a heart decision.

God looks at a person's heart. When Samuel was looking among Jesse's sons, he was reminded what his focus should be for a new king.

*The LORD does not look at the things man looks at. Man looks at the outward appearance, but the LORD looks at the heart. (1 Samuel 16:7b)*

Be encouraged. God promises that everything He asks of us is for our good.

*This commandment that I'm commanding you today isn't too much for you; it's not out of your reach... (Deuteronomy 30:11 MSG)*

*Loving God means doing what he tells us to do, and really, that isn't hard at all... (1 John 5:3 TLB)*

# Building Altars

Abraham has been a favourite Bible character of mine. In Genesis 12:1, we read of God's call on his life.

> *Go from your country, your people and your father's household to the land I will show you.*

If I had been in Abram's place, I would have been full of questions:

> *Why? Where am I going?*
> *How will I manage with all my family and animals?*
> *What will I do when I get there?*

It seems Abram didn't question God:

> *So Abram went, as the Lord had told him. (Genesis 12:4)*

The details are repeated in Hebrews 11:8,

> *...it was by faith that Abraham obeyed when God called him to leave home and go to another land, which God would give him as an inheritance. He went without knowing where he was going...*

Abram doesn't say much – no questions, no excuses, no com-

*Building Altars*

plaints. His trust in God was so strong that he was willing to do whatever God told him to do. God's proposed travel plans and all the logistics and difficulties involved, meant Abram was carrying a heavy burden.

Wherever Abram pitched his tent, instead of complaining and wanting to give up, he immediately set up an altar to God and called his people to worship.

Why an altar? It was a sacred structure, built to offer sacrifices and gifts to God. The word 'altar' is mentioned over 300 times in the Bible. Each of the four altars Abram built represented the different stages of his experience and the growth in his faith

His first altar was built (Genesis 12:7) between Shechem and Moreh. Shechem means 'a place of burden', and Moreh means 'a teacher'.

Bringing our burdens to the Lord brings us to a place of learning from Him, our teacher. Are you open to learning? It's far more productive than complaining!

Abram's second altar was between Bethel ('the house of God') and Ai ('heap of ruins') (Genesis 12:8). Have you been there? Are you found in the house of God on Sundays, then during the week your life feels as if it's in ruins? Are you trying to live as God wants you to, but life is not going as it should? When you find yourself 'between a rock and a hard place,' it's time to build another altar.

While we are admiring Abram for his faithfulness, he messes up! There is no record of God telling him to go to Egypt. We do not read of any altar built there. When Pharaoh finally throws him out of Egypt, where does Abram go? He returns to the place where he built his last altar.

*Then they continued northward toward Bethel where he had camped before, between Bethel and Ai – to the place where he*

> had built the altar. And there he again worshiped the Lord. (Genesis 13:3,4 TLB)

When we go our own way, disregarding God's leading, we need to return to where we made those wrong decisions and realign our plans with His.

In response to all that God had promised, Abram built the third altar near the oaks of Mamre, near Hebron. It was an act of thanksgiving.

> *After Lot was gone, the Lord said to Abram, 'Look as far as you can see in every direction, for I am going to give it all to you and your descendants. And I am going to give you so many descendants that, like dust, they can't be counted. Hike in all directions and explore the new possessions I am giving you.' Then Abram moved his tent to the oaks of Mamre, near Hebron, and built an altar to Jehovah there. (Genesis 13:14-18 TLB)*

Too often, we forget to be thankful. Sometimes it is a 'sacrifice of thanksgiving' when it doesn't come easily.

Finally, the last altar Abram built was where God tested his obedience by asking him to sacrifice his son.

> *Take with you your only son – yes, Isaac whom you love so much – and go to the land of Moriah and sacrifice him there as a burnt offering upon one of the mountains which I'll point out to you! (Genesis 22:2 TLB)*

Abraham learned life's most important lesson. We never fully understand faith until we realise that true worship involves surrendering all that is dear to us.

## Building Altars

All those earlier altars of sacrifice – surrender and faith – had been preparing Abraham for the moment when God would call on him to make the supreme sacrifice. So, when it came to Mt. Moriah, Abraham had a track record with God that enabled him to step out in faith and surrender.

How is your track record with God? I am reminded of some words from Wendell Smith's song, 'Come Build an Altar'.

*I came to the gathering of the people of the Lord*
*And found my way among them to His Throne*
*I needed to return to the altar of my God*
*To renew again my covenant with Him*
*And there I built an altar to His Name*
*And realised my life would never be the same*
*And then the fires of revival*
*Came sweeping through my soul*
*And I touched the holy presence of my God*

Following the earthquakes in Canterbury, we had an abundance of broken bricks. We took some to our Women's Retreat that year. After talking about Abraham and his journey, we were challenged to take a broken brick and begin to build an altar. As our 'altar' grew, it represented our broken, earthquake-damaged homes, and our broken dreams and broken lives.

As we gathered before that altar, for many, it became a place of recommitment.

Do you know the blessing of building an altar?

Do you need to renew your commitment and be prepared to lay everything at the feet of Jesus?

# Quit Quarrelling

*Quit quarrelling with God! Agree with him, and you will have peace at last! His favour will surround you if you will only admit that you were wrong. Listen to his instructions and store them in your heart. If you return to God and put right all the wrong in your home, then you will be restored. If you give up your lust for money and throw your gold away, then the Almighty himself shall be your treasure; he will be your precious silver!*

*Then you will delight yourself in the Lord and look up to God. You will pray to him, and he will hear you, and you will fulfil all your promises to him. Whatever you wish will happen! And the light of heaven will shine upon the road ahead of you. If you are attacked and knocked down, you will know that there is someone who will lift you up again. Yes, he will save the humble and help even sinners by your pure hands. (Job 22:21-30 TLB)*

**Quit quarrelling with God –**
How do we quarrel with God? Does it mean we can't ask questions? We certainly can, but quarrelling is when we disagree and want our way. If we don't get the answer we want, it can bring out a stubborn attitude when we are unwilling to change or accept His ways.

**Admit you are wrong –**
Are you brave enough to admit when you've messed up? I like the way The Message has this verse:

> Come back to God Almighty, and he'll rebuild your life.

We cannot say, 'No, Lord.' Those two words don't go together. If he is Lord, then the answer is 'Yes, Lord.'

**Listen to His instructions –**
The ability to be still and listen is a lost art these days. When teaching a junior class of very active children, I encouraged them to spend five minutes each day, sitting very still and listening. It was a tedious task! But I remember the day a young boy couldn't hold back his excitement any longer. He looked at me and whispered, 'I can hear a bird.'

When we are still and listening to God, we will hear Him speak.

Too often, our time of prayer is all about what we want. Why not spend time learning to listen? Our only prayer can be the words Eli suggested to Samuel.

> Eli told Samuel, 'Go and lie down, and if he calls you, say, 'Speak, LORD, for your servant is listening.' (1 Samuel 3:9)

When we hear His instructions, we are to 'Store them in your heart.'

**Put right all the wrong in your home –**
It is easy to see what is wrong in other people's homes, but your own is the place to start. Are you brave enough to ask God to show you what needs to be put right in your home? You can

be confident that He will begin to show you, as He wants your home to be a place where He is honoured.

**Give up your lust for money –**
Job is warning us against longing for more. It's true; the more we have, the more we want. As I write this, our area is experiencing a one in a 100-year flood. On TV, a farmer was near to tears, as he told how he had lost everything.

If all your possessions were taken away and your bank account emptied, could you still rejoice, as Habakkuk did?

Read Habakkuk 3:17,18,

*Even though ... yet I will rejoice in the God of my Salvation*

*Lust for money brings trouble and nothing but trouble. Going down that path, some lose their footing in the faith completely and live to regret it bitterly ever after. (1 Timothy 6:10 MSG)*

*Be on your guard against all kinds of greed; a man's life does not consist in the abundance of his possessions. (Luke 12:15)*

Our treasure, our most valued possession, is Jesus!

Read Job 22:26-30 to see what God has in store for those who put Him first in their lives.

# Waiting for Eagles Wings

Waiting is hard.

We have spent the last twelve months waiting for the world to recover from the Covid virus. We are still waiting.

Many families were separated as they found themselves stranded in a foreign country. Their wait to be reunited with each other has been long and difficult.

Everyday living requires waiting.

Waiting for trains, subways, buses and planes. Waiting for an important phone call or for the holidays to begin.

This year we have waited for our family to return from Europe. Covid got in the way, but after three attempts, they finally arrived in New Zealand. The waiting and uncertainty seemed endless.

We get impatient when waiting in a long checkout line at the supermarket. Our frustration level goes up when waiting for a green light at the intersection. We love the changing seasons, but the wait for winter to end can be tedious.

Waiting can be stressful.

We like the feeling of being in control of our lives. Having to wait for something or someone brings uncertainty, which takes away our control of the situation. We become more aware of the passing of time and get frustrated at wasting the time we have.

How often have you waited for something, only to find when you were finally able to have it, it was not important after all!

# Waiting for Eagles Wings

Scripture has a lot to say about waiting.

*But those who wait for the Lord [who expect, look for, and hope in Him] will gain new strength and renew their power; They will lift up their wings [and rise up close to God] like eagles [rising toward the sun]; they will run and not become weary, they will walk and not grow tired. (Isaiah 40:31 AMP)*

'Our times are in His hands.' He is in control; therefore, we must wait for the Lord. Do we wait with a sense of expectation and hope? That's when we will find our strength and power renewed. What a contradiction to our belief that waiting makes us weary and useless!

Few birds can look directly at the sun. The eagle knows that, so it flies straight towards the sun when it is being pursued by an enemy. Whatever is following it eventually gives up the pursuit.

Eagles fly to great heights by positioning their wings to soar on the air currents. They don't flap, but rather soar effortlessly.

Why does scripture compare waiting on the Lord to eagles flying high? Birds usually fly to find shelter away from a storm, but not the eagle. They love a storm and 'lift their wings' to fly directly into it, soaring to even greater heights, to eventually get above the storm.

Why should we be prepared to wait? God has the bigger picture in mind, while we see only the immediate situation. We need to wait for His timing, which is perfect. He wants nothing but the best for us.

*'For I know the plans I have for you,' declares the Lord, 'plans to prosper you and not to harm you, plans to give you hope and a future.' (Jeremiah 29:11)*

> 'For My thoughts are not your thoughts, nor are your ways My ways,' says the Lord. 'For as the heavens are higher than the earth, so are My ways higher than your ways, and My thoughts than your thoughts.' (Isaiah 55:8-9)

How should we wait? Waiting is something we can control.

> Be still before the Lord and wait patiently for him. (Psalm 37:7a)

> Wait patiently for the LORD; be brave and courageous. Wait patiently for the LORD. (Psalm 27:14)

Patience – now that is something I need a continuous supply of. It seems to allude me far too often.

To wait patiently requires us to make a choice. Can you choose to trust God, knowing His timing is perfect?

# Tangiwai and Tears

Christmas Eve, 1953. My brothers and I were in bed, supposedly asleep, but instead wide awake and excited about the next day – a day we were to celebrate Christmas at my grandparent's home, with the extended family.

Little did we know that, at 10.21 pm that night, an event happened which would have an enormous impact on our Christmas Day.

The Wellington–Auckland night express left Wellington full of passengers eager to get home for Christmas Day. Included among those passengers was a friend of my grandparents, who had recently stayed with them.

As the train approached the Whangaehu River, the driver was unaware that a mudflow from Mt Ruapehu had weakened the bridge. It collapsed as the train crossed it, plunging carriages into the flooded river, resulting in the loss of 151 lives. Known as the Tangiwai Disaster, it continues to be New Zealand's worst railway accident.

Memories are vivid of the family gathered around the radio on Christmas Day, listening to the horrific report of the night's tragedy. As a child, I was upset to see my grandfather struggling with the tears that threatened to engulf us all. He was such a strong man. The only other time I saw him on the verge of tears was years later when he lost his life's partner. Grandma passed away in her 80's.

I grew up during the years when it was said: 'boys don't cry!'

Thankfully these views are changing, but it is still the thinking of so many.

Charles Dickens wrote the following in *Great Expectations*,

*Heaven knows we need never be ashamed of our tears, for they are rain upon the blinding dust of the earth, overlying our hard hearts. I was better after I had cried than before – more sorry, more aware of my own ingratitude, more gentle.*

Why are tears so important? From a physiological point of view, tears keep the eyes moist and have a role in maintaining the healthy functioning of the eyes.

What does Scripture have to say about tears?

*You have seen me tossing and turning through the night. You have collected all my **tears** and preserved them in your bottle! You have recorded every one in your book. (Psalm 56:8 TLB)*

Hidden away among my keepsakes is a small glass bottle containing a lock of my baby curls. Why was it important for my mother to preserve that memory? To her, it was precious!

Why would God 'collect all my tears and preserve them in His bottle'? Because they are precious to Him! He not only collects them, but He also records every one of them. Nothing escapes His awareness.

Are you burdened for your family or a situation that seems out of control? Is your heart heavy with a sadness that will not leave you?

*Those who sow with tears will reap with songs of joy. (Psalm 126:5)*

Jesus came to heal the brokenhearted. He also wept at times. He wept at the loss of his friend Lazarus (John 1:35). He wept over Jerusalem and the things that were happening there (Luke 13:34). He wept as He faced His own death (Hebrews 5:7).

A recent post on Facebook was about a student having a tough day. The teacher asked if she could give her a 60-second hug. When asked: 'Why 60 seconds?' The teacher replied, 'So my heart can talk to your heart'.

God wants to talk to us amidst our tears. He cares and longs to hold us tight.

*It's ok to beat your fists against His chest. He will hold you until you feel the beat of his broken heart.*

# Get Out of Your Boat!

'Get out of your boat!' What could that mean?

It all began at a Women's Retreat when our speaker asked us to draw a picture in stages. You may like to try it yourself.

1. *Draw a scene representing your life at the moment.* Things were going well, so I drew some hills, valleys, a lake – a tranquil setting.
2. *Put yourself in the picture.* Feeling very relaxed, I drew myself in a boat out on the lake.
3. *Where is God in your picture?* I felt He was sitting in the boat with me – all was well in my world.
4. *What is He saying to you?* With such clarity, I heard the words, 'Get out of your boat.' Suddenly life was not so comfortable.

What did it mean to 'get out of my boat'? I had no idea, but I kept asking. Imagine my surprise when during the following week, a brochure arrived in the mail, advertising John Ortberg's book, *If You Want to Walk on Water You Need to Get Out of the Boat.*

That was a book I needed to buy! When it arrived, I read it cover to cover. What was God saying to me about getting out of my boat?

I still didn't understand, but thoughts kept surfacing of turning an old slide show I had created, into a book. As fast as those thoughts came, I buried them. It would be a big project and an expensive one. At the time, we were on a limited salary, and I had a part-time teaching job to help us cope financially.

That job was my security – just as *in* the boat was a secure place to be. Was God asking me to give up my teaching job? Surely leaving that security and 'stepping out of the boat' would see us floundering, maybe sinking financially.

A friend I often prayed with approached me one day and said she believed I needed to give up my teaching job. Ouch! But I knew she was right.

*God doesn't ask us to do something without assuring us that He is in it with us.*

And then another miracle. A friend was asked if she would take on a part-time job looking after a neighbour's children until the end of the year. She agreed but felt she didn't need the money – she had her children at home, so it wasn't much effort to have a few more. She rang and said she would like to give me the money she earned during that time.

Our God will supply all your needs! Over that summer, I began working on my first book, *See the Wonder*.

Walk in His will, and He will take care of you. We have found that to be true, during over 50 years in ministry and into retirement.

With the mock-up of the book finished, I decided to 'test the waters'. An appointment with a publishing firm was encouraging – until they stated the fee for printing!

'That was an interesting exercise, but there's no way I have that sort of money!' was my immediate response.

That evening, I discovered my mother had made an appointment with a real estate agent and put her home on the market, intending to move into a retirement home. Three days later, it was sold.

Lying awake that night, I wondered about God's timing. Mum now had spare money – was I prepared to risk borrowing from her? What if the whole publishing idea was a disaster?

It turned out she was more than willing to lend the amount, so I committed to repaying it gradually over the next year. If not repaid in full by then, I would take out a bank loan to finish it. It was all repaid in six months.

Why do I tell you all this?

Because it all began years before it became a reality. There was that 'still, small voice' at the beginning, then the challenge of obedience, followed by His provision. Then came the risk-taking, followed by His amazing answers.

The life of obedience starts with one small step...

Why not try this exercise for yourself?

1. *Draw a scene representing your life at the moment.*
2. *Put yourself in the picture.*
3. *Where is God in your picture?*
4. *What is He saying to you?*

# Leaving a Legacy

I was fortunate to be raised in a Christian family. We were an average family with all the ups and downs of family life.

My parents cleared some land in Taranaki, felling the trees and building a corrugated iron home among the tree stumps. They worked hard on the land, supported the local church, and raised three children, instilling in us all work ethics and Christian values.

I also had a heritage of godly grandparents. Christmas Day was a special time at their home. The dinner table was ladened with food. To our delight, Grandma always hid some coins in the Christmas pudding. It was fun to find them, but as we got older, we noticed the missionary box placed strategically in the centre of the table! The unspoken expectation was that we might give our coins to support the missionaries.

Presents surrounded the Christmas tree, but every year, before we could open them, Grandad would repeat the Christmas story of a baby born in a manger, who later died on a cross, to save each one of us.

I have no recollection of any gifts I received on Christmas Day, but I remember hearing the Christmas story and giving to the missionaries. What a legacy those generations left to their children and grandchildren.

What will your legacy be?

What do you want people to say about you when you're gone? What life story are you writing that will be left for generations to come? Will your children and grandchildren have special memories of your life? Knowing what you'd like your legacy to be can give clarity and purpose to how you live your life now.

It can be a small act of kindness done without reward or recognition that leaves a special memory.

We spent two days in Dubai en route to Europe. We had lunch at a food mall just hours before our next flight. As we were only able to exchange notes for the following currency we'd need, we counted out our remaining coins to buy a cold drink. Finding we didn't have enough to cover the cost (and not wanting to break into another note), we ordered water instead. To our surprise, the waiter placed two large orange juices in front of us. When we paid the bill, we were told there was no charge for the cold drinks. A young couple at the table next to us had overheard our conversation and had bought the drinks for us. They had left, so we were unable to thank them. When I think of Dubai, it's not the amazing sights we saw that first come to mind. It's the generosity of two strangers who gave without needing recognition.

Can you recall the names of people who influenced you and helped shape your life? During my teenage years, I was fortunate to hear two speakers who significantly impacted me.

**Gladys Aylward**: A tiny woman who had a dream – to go from England to China and work as a Christian missionary. When war broke out with Japan, Gladys gathered up 100 orphans, some of whom she had adopted, and led them on a 12-day trek into the mountains to the safety of a government orphanage at Xian. Her dream led her to the other side of the world and eventually into imminent danger, but she remained committed to her calling.

**Elizabeth Elliot**: In 1954, the Auca tribe in Ecuador killed Elizabeth's husband Jim and four other missionaries. Less than two years later, Elizabeth and her young daughter returned to live with the tribe that had murdered their loved ones. They extended forgiveness to the members of the tribe and led them to a knowledge of Jesus.

There is One who left the most incredible legacy of all – Jesus Christ. He left a gift of love, forgiveness and salvation.

*For this, you were called: because Christ also suffered for you, leaving you an example, that you should follow his steps. (1 Peter 2:21)*

He is the example we must follow if we are to leave a meaningful legacy.

# A Voice in the Night

We spent a year travelling the length of New Zealand, visiting churches. Each Sunday, my husband, Jim, preached in a different church. His message for the churches came from Psalm 134,

> *Praise the Lord, all you servants of the Lord, who minister by night in the house of the Lord. (Verse 1)*

The priests on night shift were responsible for the tasks behind the scenes. They baked the Show Bread, polished the candlesticks, cleaned the laver where the daytime priests washed. They checked the building to make sure nothing dangerous or defiling got past the gatekeepers.

The buildings were dark and empty. Nothing of consequence happened at night. Meanwhile, the day priests paraded before the crowds in their gowns and tassels. That's where God's blessing was.

But the Psalmist encouraged the night workers to recognise that the Lord knew about them and the work they were doing. They were to praise Him.

Have you found yourself serving in a place that no one knows about? Doing a task no one is aware of? Feeling lonely and unrewarded? Are you doing something that seems of no consequence?

*A Voice in the Night*

Did you know God planned your ministry tasks before you were born?

*For we are God's workmanship, created in Christ Jesus, to do good works which God prepared for us in advance to do. (Ephesians 2:10)*

If God prepared your area of ministry in advance, then He wants you there, praising Him. Even if it feels like you are serving as 'a voice in the night', He can use you to achieve great things.

Jesus' ministry could be described as a 'voice in the night'. There were the crowds who followed Him, but in the end, the skies grew dark, and Jesus cried out, 'My God, my God, why have you forsaken me?'

The disciples were discouraged as they walked along the Emmaus Road, recalling all that Jesus had done. Had it all been a waste of time? Then a stranger walked beside them, and they experienced the living Lord, encouraging them, empowering them to go to the dark, discouraging, unreceptive places, to share the story of God's grace.

*God can do anything, you know – far more than you could ever imagine or guess or request in your wildest dreams! He does it not by pushing us around but by working within us, his Spirit deeply and gently within us. (Ephesians 3:20,21 MSG)*

In those places where no one expects anything of consequence to happen, God is at work.

Elizabeth and Constantine Lewshenia were Russian radio programmers who served with HCJB in Quito, Ecuador. Following World War Two, they were involved with radio broadcasts to

Russia. During the Cold War, churches were illegal, Pastors were forbidden, and there were scarcely any Bibles.

The broadcasting team received virtually no feedback but faithfully kept broadcasting the good news of God's amazing grace. Reading the Bible passages slowly enabled the listeners to write them down. They were 'voices in the night' for over 40 years, often wondering if anything of consequence was happening.

At HCJB, broadcasts in other languages received hundreds of responses each week. But nothing from behind the Iron Curtain.

At the end of the Cold War, the Lewshenia's visited Russia. What they saw and heard amazed them. In churches and on the streets, they didn't need to be introduced. People recognised their voices. Many shared with tears how the ministry had given them hope and life.

They discovered there were over 20,000 'radio churches' formed during the 44-year-long Cold War. All over Russia, lives were transformed as people by the thousands had gathered around their radios.

Like priests ministering in the night, the HCJB team had continued serving without knowing if anything of consequence was happening.

Are you involved in a ministry where you get very little recognition? Most of us want to see results quickly. Could you wait 40 years, or would you give up, convincing yourself that nothing was happening?

Psalm 134 continues,

*Lift up your hands in the sanctuary and praise the Lord. May the Lord bless you from Zion, he who is the Maker of heaven and earth. (Verses 2-3)*

*A Voice in the Night*

If you are working the 'night shift', feeling alone and useless, be encouraged. God sees what you are doing and will bless you!

*So dear brothers and sisters, be strong and immovable. Always work enthusiastically, for you know that nothing you do for the Lord is ever useless. (1 Corinthians 15:58 NLT)*

Cast all your anxiety on Him, because He cares for you.    1 Peter 5:7

# Adopted Into the Family

Papers are signed, preparations are made, the nursery is ready, a teddy bear sits in the cot, waiting. Then the phone call comes, and the adoption process comes to fruition.

So many emotions are involved in the adoption journey. There is the difficult decision and the anguish of separation the birth mother feels.

The adopting parents have experienced loss with the inability to have their own child, maybe including several miscarriages. Then comes the legal process and the waiting for news of a suitable match. There can be weeks, months, maybe years of waiting.

When the phone call comes, and the waiting is over, the joy is indescribable – a sense of fulfilment and a commitment to nurturing this child through the years ahead.

Adoption is the 'act of leaving one's natural family and entering into the privileges and responsibilities of another'.

Ephesians 1:5 speaks about being adopted into God's family.

*Long before he laid down earth's foundations, he had us in mind, had settled on us as the focus of his love, to be made whole and holy by his love. Long, long ago, he decided to adopt us into his family through Jesus Christ. (What pleasure he took in planning this!) He wanted us to enter into the celebration of his lavish gift-giving by the hand of his beloved Son. (MSG)*

Do you know you are the 'focus of His love'? Do you experience the 'lavish gift-giving' that comes from belonging to God's family?

Adoption is the gift of being loved, of belonging, of being equal.

> *God's Spirit touches our spirits and confirms who we are. We know who He is, and we know who we are: Father and children. And we know we are going to get what's coming to us – an unbelievable inheritance! (Romans 8:17 MSG)*

Our nephew and his wife adopted a child from a Russian orphanage. Leaving the pain and loneliness behind, they took a small girl into a loving home. Imagine being an orphan, waiting at the door, feeling a sense of hope of being accepted into a family. Your new father is coming to claim you.

Our Father is coming again to take His children home, and what an inheritance awaits us.

It's a privilege to belong to a family, with all the quirks, differences, embarrassing moments and frustrations involved. What a privilege to pray for your family, knowing God loves them even more than you do!

God is interested in what may seem the insignificant details of family life and has a way of bringing everyone's plans into line.

We were faced with a dilemma when moving from an Auckland church to Te Awamutu.

Our son was chosen to play rugby with a provincial team involved in the National Championships. To our dismay, the competitions were to be held during the school holidays when we were due to move. Before we could change our plans, we waited for confirmation as to where the event was to be held, usually in a major New Zealand city.

After school one day, our boy came bursting in the door, saying, 'Guess where the Championships are going to be?' Judging by his excitement, we presumed it would be in Hamilton, just half an hour from our new church in Te Awamutu. With a sigh of relief, we knew we could make that work.

But no, it wasn't to be Hamilton. They had chosen Te Awamutu as the venue for that year's event. Consequently, we spent the first week in our new town, standing in the mud and rain, watching rugby games! During the week, his team played against the local team and he was able to make some good friends, which was a great help settling into a new school.

*In everything you do, put God first, and he will direct you and crown your efforts with success. (Proverbs 3:6 TLB)*

# Relinquishing a Dream

'You will have the desire of your heart, but it won't be easy.' Those words were spoken over me just a week before our second child was born. Convinced that we would have a girl, I bought pink wool and began knitting! As far as it not being easy – I thought that meant maybe I wouldn't be well.

Sunday 2nd September 1973 at St Helen's hospital, Wellington, our little girl was born. The following day a nurse asked me to sign a paper permitting her transfer to the Intensive Care Unit at Wellington Public Hospital. Our baby was very ill. Below my window, I saw the ambulance, engine running, ready to leave, just waiting on my signature. 'Would I see her again?'

In 1973 it was standard practice to have up to a week in the hospital, so I stayed, feeling perfectly well but with no baby! Sometime during that week, we learnt our girl had been born with meningitis. After waiting nearly a week, we were allowed to visit and were promised we could hold her. But no, that was not allowed, but at least we did see her in the incubator. Two weeks later, there was no improvement in her condition.

It was heartbreaking to see her daily, in a hospital cot, not knowing if she would live. How do you cope when life throws you a curveball? When your dreams are about to come crashing down?

During this time, I had been reading through Genesis and the story of Abraham (Genesis 22:1-19). He also had a long-awaited child whom he loved dearly.

Why would God ask him to sacrifice Isaac? Why promise him a son, only to take him away?

Abraham was a man of great faith, and he trusted God to know what was best. But he had to make that choice to obey. It was not until Abraham lifted the knife that God said: 'Stop.' Challenged by the story of Abraham, I asked myself: 'Would I be prepared to make such a sacrifice?'

The doctor had told me there was nothing more they could do for our daughter. The next day, as I stood beside the cot in the hospital, instead of asking for her healing, I found myself praying: 'Lord, it's OK if you want to take her back.' That would be the hardest thing I've ever done! But rather than feeling despair, I felt an incredible peace.

When I received a call from the hospital two days later, I braced myself to hear the news that God had taken her home. Instead, I heard she had turned a corner and could be discharged! Nurses came with tears to say goodbye. The doctor said it was a miracle, as he never expected her to leave the hospital. Not alive anyway! Our miracle baby has never looked back! At the time of writing, she is working in Switzerland for the World Health Organisation.

Why does God test us, often to the limit of what we can handle?

Why does He ask us to relinquish our dreams?

It's because He loves us and wants us to grow in our faith and trust.

The Message translation of Genesis 17:1 reads:

*God showed up.*

When there seemed no answer to the problem Abraham faced, God showed up. He will show up for you too.

*Wherever He Leads*

When God pushes you to the edge of difficulty, trust Him fully. Because two things can happen: either He'll catch you when you fall, or He'll teach you to fly!

*He knows the way that I take; when he has tested me, I will come forth as gold. (Job 23:10)*

# Are You Tired and Worn Out?

> *Burnout is a state of emotional, physical, and mental exhaustion caused by excessive and prolonged stress. It occurs when you feel overwhelmed, emotionally drained, and unable to meet constant demands.*

We can become involved with a new task and initially feel satisfaction with plenty of energy. As the stress builds up, we begin to find some days are more complicated than others. If we ignore the signs, we find ourselves becoming tired and worn out. Too much stress over a long time is not good for our physical or mental health and can lead to burnout.

Some questions worth asking yourself:

*Why do I feel proud when I tell others how busy I am?*
*Have I learnt how to say 'no' to things that will drain my energy?*
*Do I have good boundaries in my life?*

God created you, and God created time. Then He put the two of you together, giving you all the time you need, for all He wants you to do.

If you are constantly claiming you have no time, then maybe you are doing something He never intended you to do.

There are many reasons why we feel tired and stressed. There is the mother with three or four young children, who wonders if she will ever get a good night's sleep again. Or the student who studies long into the night to pass a test. A husband who works at two jobs so he can provide for his family. The Christian who runs from one meeting to another, only to find their home life is under stress.

> 'Are you tired? Worn out? Burned out on religion? Come to me. Get away with me, and you'll recover your life. I'll show you how to take a real rest. Walk with me and work with me – watch how I do it. Learn the unforced rhythms of grace. I won't lay anything heavy or ill-fitting on you. Keep company with me, and you'll learn to live freely and lightly.' (Matthew 11:28-30 MSG)

Are you tired and worn out? Are you burned out from work, studies, family life, people's expectations, unrealistic commitments? (You can probably add to the list.) In Matthew, we have three very personal questions, followed by an invitation! 'Come to me ... and recover your life.'

*Get away with me.* Have you ever taken the time to be alone with God? An hour or two just spent listening for His word to you personally? You will never regret the time spent in this way.

*I'll show you how to take a real rest.* On our way to visit my parents many years ago, our car skidded in some gravel, swerved and ended up on its side in a ditch. It took hours to deal with the aftermath, but we eventually made it to my parents' home. I still remember relaxing into the comfort of a warm bed as I let go of the day's stress. On the bedroom wall was a framed text, 'I will give you rest.' I reflected that real rest comes from letting go of all that burdens me and sinking into the comforting arms of a loving Saviour. Turn to God, and He will give you real rest.

*Walk with me and work with me.* The invitation is to walk with Him, not to run ahead or lag behind. Do I work *for* Him or *with* Him? We will become tired and stressed if we are focused on working for Him, but walking with Him gives us energy and enthusiasm. If that relationship is missing, then it's time to refocus and learn the 'unforced rhythms of grace.'

*Watch how I do it.* Jesus set us the perfect example. He knew what His mission was. Not needing anyone else's approval, He kept His attention focused on the work God gave him.

*Learn the unforced rhythms of grace.* Our lives follow natural rhythms through the seasons, years, months, weeks and days. It is a repeated pattern of how we live. Our heart and lungs follow a repeated rhythm for our lifetime. Nothing is forced. It all occurs naturally.

Following the 'rhythms of grace' is not so easy. It does not come naturally but is a choice. Grace can be described as **G**reat **R**iches **A**t **C**hrist's **E**xpense. We have done nothing to deserve the grace of God – it is a gift He offers. Through His grace, we are loved, forgiven, adopted into His family and empowered to serve. We must learn the rhythm of coming to rest in Him and receiving His grace to go out and live with Him. The struggles and stresses of life are eased as we walk in His grace.

*I won't lay anything heavy or ill-fitting on you.* The NIV says, 'my yoke is easy, and my burden is light.'

A yoke is a piece of wood tied across the necks of two oxen. It enables them to walk close to each other and work in unison. We are 'yoked' together with Jesus. He promises not to lay anything heavy on us. When we are walking in the 'unforced rhythms of grace', any burden we carry will be light if carried in unison with Him.

*Keep company with me, and you'll learn to live freely and lightly.* If you are asked to keep someone company, you will walk at their pace, focused on their wishes. Jesus wants us to move at His pace, following His plans. The burdens we carry are to be handed over to Him.

As you face a world torn apart by wars and pandemics, you need to know what it is to live freely and lightly. Living with stress and carrying heavy burdens is not God's plan for you.

# Tested by Fire

*He will sit as a refiner and purifier of silver. (Malachi 3:3a)*

This verse puzzled some women in my Bible study group. They wondered what it meant about the character and nature of God. I offered to find out about the process of refining silver and gold.

I called a goldsmith and made an appointment to watch him at work. Nothing was mentioned about the reason for my interest beyond curiosity about the process of refining gold.

He said: *'It's hard to explain the process. Only as you see it happening can you begin to understand it.'*

How true. It's as you experience God's hand in your life, that you can look back and understand it!

The following are notes I made as I watched:

- The river was dredged. There was a significant amount in the tray, but only a tiny bit of gold. The Refiner only picked out the pieces that had potential.
- He then weighed them so he could compare them with the finished pieces.
- The gold was melted in a large container, with steady bubbling at a constant temperature. As the gold settled, it became separated from any impurities. To make sure there was no gold floating in the liquid, it was diluted with water, bringing a violent reaction as the last of the gold settled.
- It was then poured into a slab where it had the potential to

harden quickly, but a certain amount of heat kept it soft and pliable.
- A sample was drilled from the gold and tested to see if anything needed adding or removing. Then once again, it was melted in a container.
- There were soon fine granules of gold, which to my untrained eye looked perfect, but I discovered the actual refining was still to come.
- All those beautiful granules of gold were poured back into the direct heat of a furnace.
- After time (only the Refiner could tell how long), the gold was poured down a long tube into cold water. This process was called the 'drag out'. It flattened the gold, giving a more extensive surface area for the cleansing action to work. The pieces, stretched so thin, now looked like cornflakes.
- The gold dropped to the bottom of the water tube. If any pieces were not a perfect shape, they were put back in the furnace, and the process repeated until the Refiner was satisfied they were perfect.

At this point, I asked, 'Is there a temptation to let some pieces slip through?'

His reply was, *'There's something about working with gold. You know you've got the best there is, and you're going to make sure the final product is perfect.'*

Finally, the gold was weighed again. With all the impurities gone, it weighed less but was worth so much more!

Why not read through those stages again – this time in the light of Isaiah 48:10,

*'I refined you in the furnace of affliction.' (TLB)*

God refines those with the potential to be changed. It takes the heat of affliction to separate us from the impurities in our lives. This process may well cause a violent reaction in us!

> *I myself, will melt you in a smelting pot, and skim off your slag...* (Isaiah 1:25 TLB)

Only God knows how long our refining will take.

There are times when we are stretched to our limit and our 'refining' is dragging on too long, but it is so necessary for the cleansing to continue. Often, to our dismay, the process needs to be repeated.

God knows us and wants nothing but the best for us. He knows how much heat we can take. He carefully watches over us.

> *He must become greater; I must become less.* (John 3:30)

At the end of the process, the beauty of the gold was amazing. I was reminded of how much care our loving Father takes as He deals with us. His refining process is meant for our good.

And the outcome?

> *But he knows the way that I take, when he has tested me, I will come forth as gold.* (Job 23:10)

# Wearing a Mask

How often are you asked, 'How are you?' only to carefully adjust your mask and reply, 'I'm fine, thanks.'

During the Covid pandemic, face masks became a familiar sight. They were necessary for our protection, and before long, people became used to wearing them.

For most of us, we had been wearing invisible masks long before the pandemic. We hide behind false smiles, headphones or even dark glasses. Why do we feel they are necessary?

We tend to think people don't care. If someone asks how we are doing, we perceive they are asking out of politeness. We smile and answer 'fine', even though we may be hurting and disappointed.

Gossip, at some time, has probably affected all of us. It can leave us reluctant to confide in others for fear of how far they may spread our story. So, our mask is firmly in place for our protection.

There are many masks available to us. The mask of 'I've got it all together' or 'I don't need anyone'. We can wear the mask of busyness, projecting how important we are and that we don't have time for others.

We shuffle our masks on and off from one situation to another until one day, our cover fails us. No matter how good you are at the game, eventually cracks develop, and people start to see the real you.

Being the real you is the best you can be. Oscar Wilde once said, 'Be yourself; everyone else is taken.'

*Wearing a Mask*

Be proud of who you are. You are unique.

*I praise you, for I am fearfully and wonderfully made. (Psalm 139:14)*

Unfortunately, because we are so used to wearing a mask, we are too proud to admit it isn't the real me, so we create even more masks.

Have you ever asked someone to fix a broken ornament yet held back some of the pieces? Unless every piece is available, the ornament can never be completely put together.

How can we help others to unmask?

- First of all, be prepared to remove your own mask. It can make you vulnerable, but others will see you as genuine.
- Be trustworthy. If someone is prepared to let down their mask, they need to know they have your confidentiality.
- Be available. Make time to develop honest relationships, even if it means shifting our priorities and changing our over-committed schedules.
- Be a good listener, use eye contact, and don't interrupt. Respond to their needs with compassion.

In Scripture, there are many verses about how we are to treat each other.

*Bear with each other... (Colossians 3:13)*

*Therefore encourage one another and build each other up... (1 Thessalonians 5:11)*

*Love one another deeply, from the heart... (1 Peter 1:22b)*

*Accept one another... (Romans 15:7)*

How can others support us if we mask our pain and pretend to be fine?

When we first moved to the Far North of New Zealand, we were amused to see two signs for the same area. At the boundary between Auckland and Northland, there was a sign, 'Welcome to the Far North'. But 100 kilometres further on was another sign, 'Welcome to the REAL Far North.'

Do we need a sign around our necks, 'Welcome to the Real Me'?

Think about the masks you wear. Is it time to take them off? You are a unique person, with gifts to offer the world. Don't miss those opportunities by hiding them behind a mask.

# A Day to Remember

There are days each of us have etched in our memory: the good and the bad. In Matthew chapter 14, we read of a day Peter would never forget. A day out fishing on the lake ended up battling a storm and then an encounter with Jesus.

Where was Jesus?

He was alone in the hills. As the men struggled to keep their boat afloat, they no doubt wondered where Jesus was. If ever they needed Him, it was now. He'd been with them in their boat one other time during a storm. Had He forgotten them this time?

We all experience those days when the storm is too big, the task too great, the future too bleak, the answers too few. Sometimes on those days, we constantly ask, 'Where is Jesus in all this mess?'

We toss and turn during the night, with a thousand questions on our mind. I'm encouraged to read Jesus came to the disciples at 3 am. During those long night hours, when we wrestle with our storms, Jesus is there. We can safely leave the night time with Him.

When Jesus finally turned up, the disciples didn't recognise Him. He may turn up when you least expect it. If you are not looking for Him, you might miss Him.

As they looked out across that stormy sea, something in Peter recognised Jesus. In his usual impetuous way, he called out:

*'Lord, if it's you ... tell me to come to you on the water.'*
*(Matthew 14:28)*

Before Peter stepped out of the boat, he needed to make sure that Jesus thought it was a good idea too!

Put yourself in Peter's place. It was pitch black, the waves were crashing, gale-force winds were battering their boat, and they were all exhausted. It would be tough enough to walk on water on a calm sunny day, but in these conditions?

What would you choose, the water or the boat? If I'd been there, the conversation would have gone like this: 'Lord, why don't you do something about this storm? Then we can talk.'

Yet Peter sensed that Jesus was inviting him to take a step of faith. His heart must have been pounding as he put a foot over the side of the boat. Would Jesus be there for him? As he leaves the ship's relative safety, he abandons himself utterly to Jesus' care.

Then – 'he saw the wind.' But hadn't the wind been there all the time? When stepping out of the boat, Peter's focus had been on Jesus, but then he became aware of the wind.

Often, once the decision is made to take a step of faith, reality sets in: 'What have I done?'

Keep your eyes focused on Jesus.

*Fixing **our eyes on Jesus** ...so that you will not grow weary and lose heart. (Hebrews 12:2-3)*

We may be tempted to criticise Peter. Was he too impetuous? Was he a failure? There is one thing sure – Peter stepped out of the boat, while the other disciples stayed in the boat, cowering from the storm. Peter was the only one who knew what it was to walk on water, experiencing the thrill of taking Jesus' hand and being rescued in his time of desperate need.

Jesus is always 'out on the water', calling us to join Him in a life of adventure. Are you desperately hanging on, wondering whether you can trust God to be there for you, if you let go?

### The Trapeze

*I feel like a trapeze artist high above the earth*
*Knuckles white, as I grip the bar,*
*wishing I was somewhere else.*
*You throw me a new bar, it swings towards me so close...*
*Yet too far away to reach without letting go*
*of the bar I'm holding.*
*Lord, I'm afraid. It would be so much easier if I could go back*
*to where I was,*
*But I can't, I'm already committed to going forward.*

*This bar I'm holding is my security;*
*I've got to let it go and risk*
*if I'm to know the thrill of flying with You.*
*I hear your voice urging me to let go, to risk it, to trust You.*
*Your hands reach out to me,*
*The look in your eyes gives me confidence.*

*You have caught me before will you catch me again?*
*Despite my fear, my apprehension,*
*I'll let go and trust you, Lord.*

*– Author unknown*

# Earthquakes and Aftershocks

September 4, 2010, 4:35 am – a date and hour etched on our memory! Living in the rural town of Darfield, we soon heard we had been at the epicentre of a 7.1 magnitude earthquake. It came in the early hours of the morning, without warning, lasting only 40 seconds, yet leaving widespread destruction. Over 11,000 aftershocks continued during the following year.

Some of our life experiences can feel like earthquakes. When all is going well, suddenly there is a situation that comes out of nowhere, takes you by surprise, and causes havoc in your life.

One thing we can be sure of in this life – we will face the unexpected. Life, like earthquakes, can be unpredictable. Trouble is going to cross our path at various times, but our peace is found in Him.

*I have told you these things, so that in Me you may have peace. In this world, you will have trouble. But take heart! I have overcome the world. (John 16:33)*

Since the 2010 earthquake and then the Christchurch earthquake five months later, we have been encouraged to have survival kits ready, should there be a repeat performance.

How often have I heard the comment: 'Yes, I have some things put aside, but I know I should be better prepared!'

How can we prepare ourselves for the day when our world turns upside down?

First of all, we need a firm belief about Who is in control.

*When the earth and all its people quake, it is I who hold its pillars firm. (Psalm 75:3)*

Surrounding every unexpected event in your life are the firm hands of a loving Father.

We need a personal relationship with God.

*One thing I ask from the LORD, this only do I seek: that I may dwell in the house of the LORD all the days of my life... For in the day of trouble he will keep me safe in his dwelling... (Psalm 27:4,5)*

Where else would you want to be on that day when troubles land at your feet? If we seek His presence in the ordinary daily routine, we will be ready and safe to face life's problems.

Make sure you are grounded in the Word of God.

A crucial factor in whether buildings withstood the 7.1 earthquake was the building materials and foundations. Our lives will withstand life's storms if our foundations are firm. What is your life founded on? What are you building into your life?

Read again the story of Paul and Silas in Acts 16:23-26,

*After they had been severely flogged, they were thrown into prison, and the jailer was commanded to guard them carefully. When he received these orders, he put them in the inner cell and fastened their feet in the stocks.*

*About midnight Paul and Silas were praying and singing hymns to God, and the other prisoners were listening to them. Suddenly there was such a violent earthquake that the foundations of the prison were shaken. At once all the prison doors flew open, and everyone's chains came loose.*

Here were two men in a prison's inner cell, their feet in stocks, with no chance of escape. They spent their time praying and singing hymns, totally focused on God, not on their problems. Others were watching and listening.

Suddenly, out of nowhere came a strong earthquake, shaking the foundations so violently, the prisoner's chains came loose!

Does your situation feel like a prison sentence with no hope of escape? Are you focused on your problems or praise and prayer? Remember, there will always be others watching you.

When your life is shaken to the core, it could well be the means of loosening some chains and setting you free!

Read 1 Samuel 30:1-6. David was deeply distressed. His home had been destroyed and his family kidnapped. David was weeping until he had no strength to cry anymore.

*David was greatly distressed... But he found strength in the LORD his God. (1 Samuel 30:6)*

In times of your most profound distress, find your strength in the Lord your God.

*God is too wise to be mistaken;*
*God is too good to be unkind*
*So when you don't understand,*
*When you don't see His plan*
*When you can't trace His hand,*
*Trust His Heart*

*– Babbie Mason*

# Doing or Being?

We often read of the comparison between Mary and Martha, followed by the question, 'Who are you?' Do we have to be one or the other? During my teenage years I was once told, 'You are a real Martha.' It was meant in a kind way, as a thank you for helping clean up after a function. Those words stayed with me for a long time, but initially I wasn't sure how to take it. Did I want to be a Martha? Being a Mary sounded a lot more spiritual!

> *As Jesus and his disciples were on their way, he came to a village where a woman named Martha opened her home to him. She had a sister called Mary, who sat at the Lord's feet listening to what he said. But Martha was distracted by all the preparations that had to be made. She came to him and asked, 'Lord, don't you care that my sister has left me to do the work by myself? Tell her to help me!'*
>
> *'Martha, Martha,' the Lord answered, 'you are worried and upset about many things, but few things are needed – or indeed only one. Mary has chosen what is better, and it will not be taken away from her.' (Luke 10:38-42)*

We meet these two women in Martha's home, where she welcomed Jesus and his disciples (and probably a lot of other followers) and began preparing a meal.

It didn't take long before she complained about her sister not helping with the work. If you've been in a similar situation, you

## Doing or Being?

will feel some sympathy for Martha. Why should she be left to do all the work, while her sister just sat around!

But Jesus gently rebuked Martha saying she was too distracted with things that were not important. Her sister Mary, had made a better choice, as she sat at Jesus' feet, listening to Him.

Every day we must make choices. Will we be a Mary or a Martha? There are times when we must be a Martha. The work needs to be done, but Jesus made it very clear what the best choice is.

It is easy to lead a life that is full of 'doing'. We rush from one commitment to another, feeling important because we are so busy. Do you have to-do lists? I do, and some days, after completing a task, I have been known to add it to the list, just to have the satisfaction of crossing it off!

The 'doers' love to set goals and achieve them. Failure can lead to frustration and depression. Jesus described Martha as being 'distracted with much serving'. She was worried and upset. There didn't seem to be a lot of joy in her choice.

We must learn to make the 'better' choice, and take time to sit at Jesus' feet. Instead of continual 'doing', there needs to be time to just 'be'.

For those who love doing rather than being, it will be hard to make the choice to *do* less and *be* more in His presence. Where else are you going to discover what His plans for you are?

Jesus commended Mary for choosing the 'one thing necessary' – listening to Him. Without hearing his instructions, we will achieve nothing.

*Whoever abides in me and I in him, he it is that bears much fruit, **for apart from me you can do nothing**. (John 15:5 ESV)*

*Wherever He Leads*

We have hands to do the work, and a heart to rest and listen.

Is Jesus inviting you to take time out of your busy schedule, and to rest at his feet, and listen to him.

# Hang in There

I wonder how many unfinished projects you have? There is a great sense of achievement when we complete what we started. Often life gets busy, and a project is set aside until a more convenient time. Sometimes that convenient time never arrives. For whatever reason, an unfinished task is never very satisfying!

In Genesis 11:31 we read:

*Terah took his son Abram, his grandson Lot son of Haran, and his daughter-in-law Sarai, the wife of his son Abram, and together they set out from Ur of the Chaldeans to go to Canaan. But when they came to Harran, they settled there.*

Terah set off to the land of Canaan but stopped at Harran and settled there. We don't know why he stopped there, but we know he never arrived at his planned destination. He started a journey he never finished. He died in Harran.

What stopped Terah from reaching his goal? Why was he prepared to settle for something less than what God had for him? The promised land of Canaan was before him, but he decided to stay in the comfort of Harran.

God has a purpose for our lives, and we need to be careful not to become comfortable and settle for less.

What if, on Judgement Day, God were to show us how different our lives would have been if we hadn't settled short of the goal? Do you want to be remembered for not quite making it, because somewhere along the way, you settled for less?

After his father died, Abram heard God's call to take up the journey again. The way of life in Harran had to be left behind. Have you become sidetracked from all God has for you? Is there a way of life that needs to be left behind?

> *Since, then, we do not have the excuse of ignorance, everything, and I do mean everything connected with that old way of life, has to go. It's rotten through and through. Get rid of it! And then take on an entirely new way of life – a God-fashioned life, a life renewed from the inside and working itself into your conduct as God accurately reproduces his character in you.*
> *(Ephesians 4:24 MSG)*

Abram receives his instructions but no definite destination.

> *The Lord had said to Abram, 'Go from your country, your people and your father's household to the land I will show you.'*
> *(Genesis 12:1)*

Our spiritual journey can be like that. It's the difference between using a map or GPS. With a map, you can plan your journey and see which route you will take; with the GPS, you rely on someone else telling you where to go.

A map can be thrown into the car's back seat when you decide to go your own way, but a GPS can be hard to ignore when it continually tells you to recalculate!

God tells us to reconnect or recalculate when we get side tracked or tempted to give up on the journey.

It's a new day, and Abram is ready to move on. How carefully did he follow God's instructions? He was told to 'go from' his country, his people and his father's household. But he took Lot and all the possessions and people they had acquired in Haran.

Partial obedience never gets you anywhere. God is looking for people who will respond with complete obedience each time He speaks. We must be willing to make the sacrifices required. Disobedience to God always brings consequences.

In the words of a hymn by John H. Sammis, 'Trust and obey, for there's no other way to be happy in Jesus but to trust and obey.' All too often, we sing this familiar hymn without giving the words much thought. Blessing comes from complete obedience to His Word.

Faith and obedience go hand in hand.

*God spoke to me today. He broke through my childish doubts with words of comfort and assurance. 'Hang in there, sit tight. Stick to My course for your life,' He said. 'I will not let you down.' (Psalm 110, L.F. Brandt, Psalms Now)*

# How Will this Journey End?

*It is good to have an end to journey toward; but it is the journey that matters in the end. – Ernest Hemingway*

Life is an exciting journey from the cradle to the grave. How we live our life will help determine how we end it. Has our focus been on gaining plenty of possessions and memorable experiences? Have we spent our time involved in many good activities, but neglected to spend quality time with family and friends?

More important than anything else, have we maintained a close relationship with Jesus? Will He welcome us one day, knowing our life has been spent in His company?

One of the certainties in this journey we are on, is that it will come to an end.

A phone call late one night, and your world falls apart.
A slow battle with sickness that takes a life too soon.
A gradual letting go of a long and well-lived life.
A long-awaited birth that results in a stillbirth.
A road accident that takes a loved one.

The circumstances may vary, but when a life is over, there is a hole that is hard to fill. As you journey through life, death will cross your path many times. It may begin with the passing of a parent. If they have lived a long life, that can be a comfort, but there is no escaping the hole left in your heart.

Why is it that we don't want to die or even talk about death?

Is it because there are so many unknowns? What will the death process be like? Will it be painful or peaceful? How will I cope with a loved one's death? Will I be strong, or will grief take over my life?

These are questions that we probably don't have answers to.

It's right to grieve. There are times when our emotions will threaten to overwhelm us – when living seems too hard.

Even various Scriptures can be confusing, but I am encouraged by 1 Thessalonians 4:13b,

> ...that you may not grieve like the rest of mankind, who have no hope.

There is the key – the presence of hope. Hope can come in various forms. When there is no hope, life and ultimately death will leave us devastated. It's worth becoming acquainted with the five stages of grief: denial, anger, bargaining, depression, and acceptance. Those stages give hope and confidence that our suffering is normal and will pass.

But our primary source of hope is found in Scripture. Our hope lies in the promises of God, knowing that heaven is the reward for those who have put their trust and belief in Christ.

> What no eye has seen, what no ear has heard, and what no human mind has conceived – the things God has prepared for those who love him. (1 Corinthians 2:9)

When your heart is overwhelmed with grief, turn again to the Scriptures.

*My flesh and my heart may fail, but God is the strength of my heart and my portion forever. (Psalm 73:26)*

*The LORD is my rock, my fortress and my deliverer; my God is my rock, in whom I take refuge... (Psalm 18:2)*

*The LORD is close to the broken-hearted and saves those who are crushed in spirit. (Psalm 34:18)*

*He heals the broken-hearted and binds up their wounds. (Psalm 147:3)*

> A broken heart can find rest
> in the healing arms of Jesus.

The well-known hymn 'It Is Well with My Soul' was written by Horatio Spafford after his four daughters died at sea, when the SS *Ville du Havre* sank while crossing the Atlantic in 1873.

Can you face your last days with the confidence that it is 'well with your soul'?

*When peace like a river attendeth my way*
*When sorrows like sea billows roll*
*Whatever my lot, Thou hast taught me to say*
*It is well. It is well with my soul.*

www.ingramcontent.com/pod-product-compliance
Lightning Source LLC
Chambersburg PA
CBHW071837290426
44109CB00017B/1834